AF269861

Take Care of Your Body

Learn about Healthy Hygiene with Sesame Street

Nicole Gabor

Lerner Publications ◆ Minneapolis

In this series, young readers will learn different ways they can take care of themselves! Come along as Elmo and his *Sesame Street* friends explore how healthy habits—like eating well and expressing your feelings—help you grow smarter, stronger, and kinder.

Sincerely,
the Editors at Sesame Workshop

Table of Contents

What Is Hygiene?

Hygiene is keeping yourself clean so that you can stay healthy. Practice healthy habits to keep clean.

Elmo loves to washy wash!

Healthy Habits

Brush your teeth every morning and night.
This keeps your mouth clean and healthy.

Brush in little circles. Go from side to side,
up and down, and front and back.

Washing your hands is one way to stay healthy! Wash them before eating, after going to the bathroom, and after playing outside.

While I wash my hands, I sing the ABCs!

Showers and baths keep your body clean and healthy.

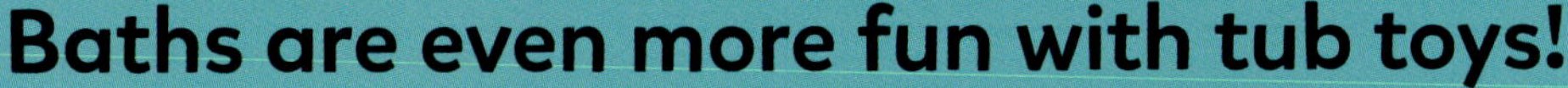

Baths are even more fun with tub toys!

If you feel a tickle in your nose or throat, sneeze or cough into your elbow.

This keeps germs from spreading.

Taking care of yourself also means going to the doctor for checkups. Doctors and nurses check to see that you are staying healthy and help you feel better when you are sick.

When I grow
up, I want to be
a doctor!

At the doctor's office, you might have to get a shot.

16

A shot hurts a little bit and feels like a quick pinch.

17

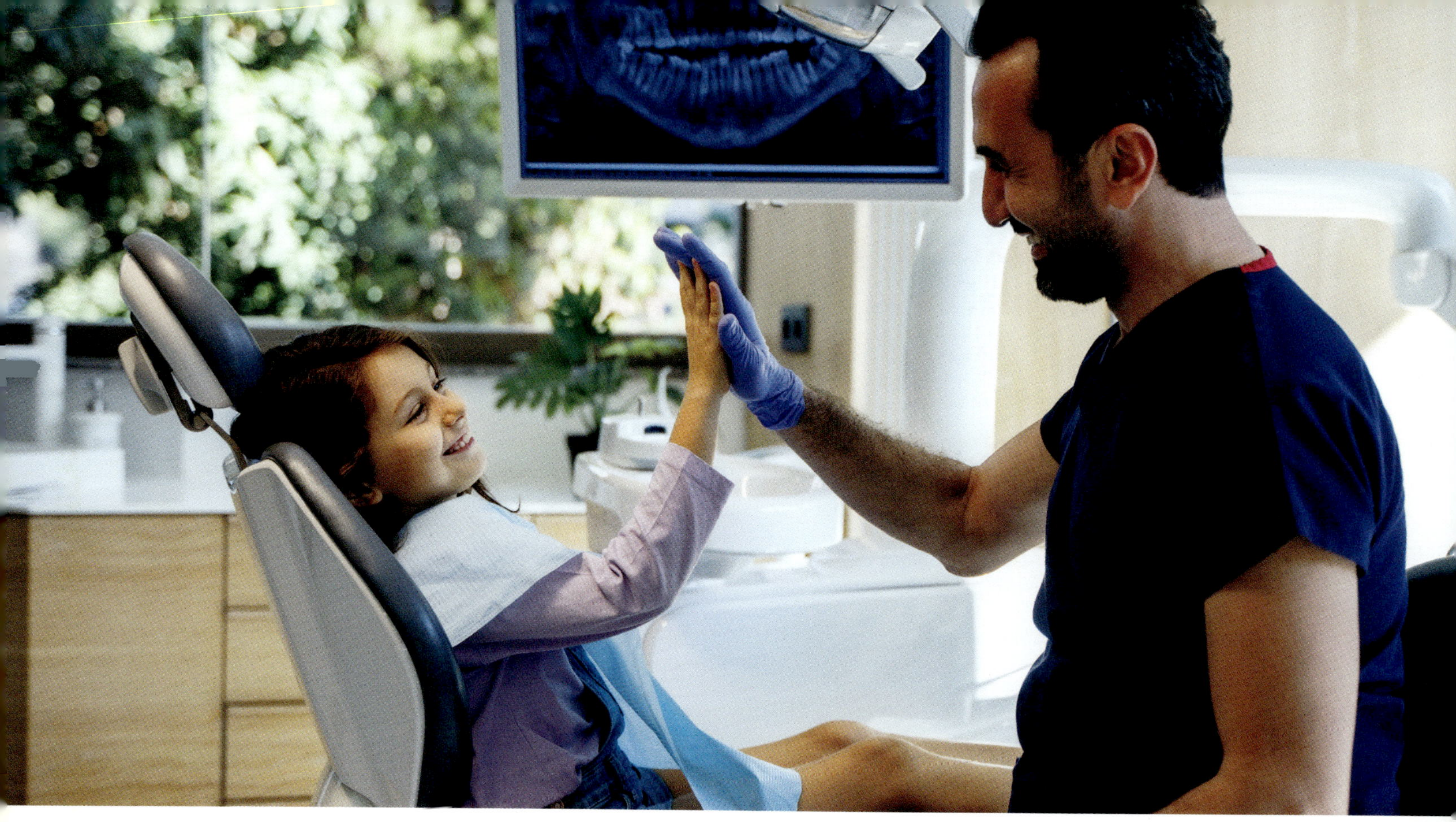

A dentist is a doctor who takes care of your teeth. Visit the dentist for a checkup to keep your teeth clean and healthy.

Dentists keep my adorable, little teeth strong.

By practicing these healthy habits, you'll have good hygiene. This helps keep you healthy and feeling your best!

A toothbrushing chart helps you remember to brush your teeth. You can create your own by making two boxes for each day. When you finish brushing your teeth in the morning, check off one of the boxes. When you finish brushing your teeth at night, check off the other box!

Glossary

checkups: visits to the doctor or dentist to check if you are healthy

dentist: a doctor who helps keep your teeth healthy

doctor: a person who helps keep people healthy

germs: very tiny things that make a person sick when they get inside the body

Read More

Murray, Julie. *Taking Care of Your Teeth*. Minneapolis: Abdo Kids, 2024.

Reynolds, Cat. *Washy Wash! And Other Healthy Habits*. New York: Random House Children's Books, 2020.

Schuh, Mari. *Taking Care of Me: Healthy Habits with Sesame Street*. Minneapolis: Lerner Publications, 2021.

Photo Acknowledgments

Image credits: Moyo Studio/Getty Images, p. 4; PeopleImages.com - Yuri A/Shutterstock, p. 7; ucchie79/Shutterstock, p. 8; MoMo Productions/Getty Images, p. 10; BSIP/Getty Images, p. 13; FatCamera/Getty Images, pp. 14, 17; ozgurdonmaz/Getty Images, p. 18; monkeybusinessimages/Getty Images, p. 20. Design elements: Dedraw Studio/Shutterstock.

Index

International copyright secured. No part of this book may be reproduced, stored in a retrieval system, or transmitted in any form or by any means—electronic, mechanical, photocopying, recording, or otherwise—without the prior written permission of Lerner Publishing Group, Inc., except for the inclusion of brief quotations in an acknowledged review.

Lerner Publications Company
An imprint of Lerner Publishing Group, Inc.
241 First Avenue North
Minneapolis, MN 55401 USA

For reading levels and more information, look up this title at www.lernerbooks.com.

Main body text set in Mikado. Typeface provided by HVD.

Designer: Laura Otto Rinne **Photo Editor:** Nicole Berglund
Lerner team: Martha Kranes

Library of Congress Cataloging-in-Publication Data

Names: Gabor, Nicole, author.
Title: Take care of your body : learn about healthy hygiene with Sesame Street / Nicole Gabor.
Description: Minneapolis, MN : Lerner Publications, [2025] | Series: Sesame Street self-care | Includes bibliographical references and index. | Audience: Ages 4–8 | Audience: Grades K–1 | Summary: "Hygiene means keeping yourself healthy and feeling your best! Alongside Sesame Street friends, young readers learn the importance of toothbrushing, bathing, handwashing, and much more"— Provided by publisher.
Identifiers: LCCN 2024006314 (print) | LCCN 2024006315 (ebook) | ISBN 9798765643686 (library binding) | ISBN 9798765658079 (epub)
Subjects: LCSH: Hygiene—Juvenile literature. | Health—Juvenile literature.
Classification: LCC RA777 .G325 2025 (print) | LCC RA777 (ebook) | DDC 613—dc23/eng/20240412

LC record available at https://lccn.loc.gov/2024006314
LC ebook record available at https://lccn.loc.gov/2024006315

ISBN 979-8-7656-6238-0 (pbk.)

Manufactured in the United States of America
1-1010917-52409-5/30/2024